Einstein's Brain

Einstein's Brain

Mark O'Flynn

PUNCHER & WATTMANN

First published in 2022
Published by Puncher and Wattmann
PO Box 279
Waratah NSW 2298

https://www.puncherandwattmann.com
web@puncherandwattmann.com

ISBN   9781922571519

Cover design and typesetting by Morgan Arnett
Printed by Lightning Source International

NATIONAL LIBRARY OF AUSTRALIA
A catalogue record for this work is available from the National Library of Australia

for Eamon

"To forgive is wisdom, to forget is genius. And easier. Because it's true. It's a new world every heart beat."
— Joyce Cary

Contents

Einstein's Brain	11
Melbourne Weather	14
Golf Balls on the Moon	16
Sea of Crises	17
Beneath the Cartouche – 1836	18
Glacier	19
In the Dunes	21
Pickers Quarters	22
Quiet Decibels	23
What We Saw in the Sky to the East	24
Funny Hat	28
Hand to Mouth	30
Interesting Times	31
Trees Without Passports	34
In the Ladies Parlour – Woodford Academy	36
Cogito Ergo Something	38
Talon	40
Hit Dog	41
The 'Riff	43
Sound Track	44
Peach Tree	45
My Ears	46
Rat Nest	47
The Hippos of Venezuela	48
Ann Hodges, 1954	50
Communion of Stones	51
Shackleton's Hut	52
Building Site	56
Monotreme	57
Silvereyes	58

Ibis   59

Turtle   60

On the Shoalhaven   61

Ludmilla's Cottage   63

The Chorus Girl   65

Soapbox Orator   71

In Case of Fire   74

Furniture Music   77

Suitcase   81

More Rhetorical Questions   82

Lines for Lyres   83

The Light Fantastic   88

Angophoras   90

Egg Beater   91

Bio Note   92

Acknowledgements   95

Einstein's Brain

Introduction:
First Ned Kelly's skull
then Pharlap's mighty heart.
Phrenology and the history of morbid awe.
Next to be purloined
for purposes of research was Einstein's brain,
(plus his eyeballs
given as a present to Albert's ophthalmologist).
The hypothesis of the current study posits the question: Why?
Supposition: Because.

Method:
With a saw.
Back and forth until the cranium popped.
Cause of death: a burst aorta.
Taken straight from the autopsy by Dr Thomas Harvey
realising who it was on the slab
and what an opportunity this might mean for science.
The brain weighing an ordinary three pounds (approx)
was kept in a pickling jar
in a cider box
under a Budweiser beer cooler
in Tom Harvey's basement
for twenty-three years.
Harvey's wife laid down an ultimatum,
it's either me or the brain.
He chose the brain.

Results:
Forensically dissected into 240 pieces
the brain became an even bigger jigsaw.
Sent out on slides to labs across the country
they counted the neurons, glia, sulci, gyri
only to find (inconclusively) there were lots.
The musical cortex, admittedly, larger.
That's what ten hours sleep a night
plus eating grasshoppers will do
which Einstein did.

Discussion:
He published nothing, Harvey.
Gave away slices of it to casual fans.
Did not sell it to the military who wanted it
in order to defeat the Russians
themselves collecting brains of their own.
Lost his medical practitioner's licence.
Found work in a plastics factory in Wichita.
Eventually returned to Princeton,
the brain in a tub in the trunk of his car,
not so much at the speed of light,
more the speed of a Buick Skylark
in heavy traffic, all things being relative.

Conclusion:
Taciturn iconoclast.
Harvey behind the wheel
getting too old to care for it now,
wanting to donate it back.
Still listening for what the silence
of the brain might have to tell him,
what esoteric secrets of the universe,
hopefully not in German which, like the nurse
who misheard Einstein's dying words,
Harvey did not speak.

Melbourne Weather

1.

Spring pries into your affairs like a witness
going through the paperwork of silence.
There is a moment when all is worth it
when memory of the ephemeral surpasses
the resolution to outlive it. Spring delves
into the mystery of one long promise
of plague: gnats, rabbits, advertising jingles.
When the spasm of blossom peers
into the world from the bract there we shall be
in ignorance of everything but our allergies.
We'll devote attention to the subjective
beauty of pollen, when each tendril unfurls
to reveal a lost love that never dies
continuing between the fire and the flies.

2.

Summer cranks up the motivation
to seek out the real-estate of shade.
A profit to be made if only
we can learn to think like the sun.
Our skin cringes under the magnifying
glass of ambition. A solstice somewhere.
We hibernate beside the air-conditioning
hoping the heat will not ignite our prayers.
Our brains rattle with cicadas, the sticks
on the ground shrivel like baked annelids.
All is cooked in the world.
One of these days summer won't stop,
everything will go up in smoke,
not one cool person will have the voice to speak.

3.

One by one the autumn leaves exhale
their last, to use a human metaphor.
Decay's work is never done in order
to establish the cycle of the seasons
intricately linked to the cycle
of everything else. To improve
would be a fiction. There must be flaws
so the system can renew. Whether
we want it to or not is another matter.
Inevitably we descend into compost,
the lacework of a rotting leaf representing
more than we'd truly care to know.
The subtlety of the colour blind
brings the end of autumn's reign to mind.

4.

Winter curls its leafless fingers
about a hot mug of chocolate
deferring to the usual words of wisdom
regarding gloves, scarves, rugging up.
If you're going to go out in it don't pretend
you're stronger than the elements.
Around any corner you might catch your death,
just as likely if you sit still indoors
watching it all unfold on the telly.
That icy air filling your suburban lungs
with the opportunity to dig your own grave
out of the backyard's snowdrift.
Lie down, relax. Winter - do your worst,
drag the soil back over you, warm as toast.

Golf Balls on the Moon

What will they think
when they come to reconnoitre
and find two Spalding Hot Dots,
or what ever commercial name
those golf balls went by,
sitting in the eternal dust?
Two of them. Hit to test
the slow-mo reach of gravity,
lost forever in the rough. One day
some Martian or other will peer
over the lunar horizon to the blue
opal floating in the void, this little
dimpled asteroid in his alien paw
and cry silently to the darkness – fore.

Sea of Crises

Regarding the moon:
Turn on the news, take your pick.
No need to be literal here. No overdue
calamity, no whirling maelstrom in the shipping
lanes, simply what to cook for dinner. What
to talk about over canapés. Most days the queue
to the checkout is enough to shatter the singing crystal
spheres. In them a single planet stopped in its tracks
once conjured witches. These epicycles
forced us to question the centre. What centre?
There is no centre. Only a perpetual
outwardness leaving us recoiling from ourselves.
All this dust and nowhere to sweep it.

Beneath the Cartouche — 1836

What have these old grey flagstones seen?
Worn like soup spoons with passing trade.
Above the Taproom portal a cartouche
of fruit and grain, fermenting overproof
cornucopia, drink up friend — welcome
if you dare. Only the slow delay of evening
before the journey on to golden dreams
sprouting in the dirt of the Turon. We'd follow
if we could, if we had the wishing.

Here at Twenty Mile Hollow
or what ever name it goes by these days,
so far from the nearest warmth
of a kindred soul, the blessing
of a loaded plate, a roof overhead, this horn
of plenty - what more could anyone ask?
Who lit that tallow candle attracting
every heathen bug in Christendom? How far must
a body travel from the moment of its birth?

What have these stone walls heard
in the accent of history's echo?
Whatever common luxury we'll pay for.
That nocturnal droning
of the interrupted songlines, to make
a home from something so foreign
as a roof. The voices trapped by clouds
floating over the merciless bush,
the language of the trees hissing in tongues.

Glacier

[– so may my words
Give shade in a land that lacks a human heart.]
– James K. Baxter

From the terminal face, the melt cascades
across the boulders tumbled smooth as grief.

The soft neve smothers everything we feel except wonder.
Down the labyrinth of moulins her sobbing torrents pour.

Back in love's ice ages mourning took forever.
Seracs splinter and drip

beneath the mythical stillness of Hinehukatere's tears
which once reached beyond the sea

shouldering gravel aside in great bluffs.
Grief retreats with a glacier's rapidity

to a shrinking precipice
but never shrinks completely.

The rising rivers gush their howling
over stone, inexorably changing course,

clawed smooth by ice peppered with rock flour.
Our camp now miles inland

where once her yearning reached
leaving icebergs and kettle lakes to drown in.

Beyond the bulldozed levee
gnawed by the glacier's slow teeth

our bed lies with the avalanche girl
grinding below the surface of the river.

In the Dunes

I have wandered the dunes
and found the shallow indentations
of two castaways at rest.
Tussocks of sword grass cling to the sand
like fingers entwined in hair,
their leaves scissoring the sky.
I have stumbled from one end
of the isthmus to the other
searching for foot prints
left by the tide.
Bones of driftwood roll
in shallows, tossing and turning
like restless insomniacs.
Small fish trapped in rock pools
remember your feet, while
the bristling urchins flaunt
crimson spears, a clattering
battle at the point of stillness.

Pickers Quarters

The only shady spot for that lone Aberdeen Angus
bull was under the crab-apple tree outside our kitchen
window. So many green apples we threw at it
till it pulled up anchor, farting sloppily, mooing
with a gut ache across the open paddock.

When the corner of the picking sack tore off
and the fastening hook plunged into my eye I
screamed twice, although my mate, Robbo,
told me it was definitely three times, third time
being the silent scream in my head made manifest.

Old Joe, the boss, a ball of muscle like a bullfrog,
looked more shocked than me at the conjunction
of eye and hook. Robbo drove me to hospital where
they discovered, still I can hardly believe it,
no major damage. Day off work.

Next morning everyone else returned to picking.
I almost grew bored throwing apples at that bull.
Mrs. Joe, the Italian mama, sat me down
at the Laminex table, changed the dressing on my eye,
counting the drops she squeezed into it, *uno,*
due, tre, her tomato sandwiches for morning tea,
the soft rain of her fingers on my face
the gentlest thing I'd felt in years.

Quiet Decibels

The next-door radio mumbles to itself.
A sudden bird flees across the roof,
a donkey on tip-toes brays in the evening distance.
Not everyone can say as much
of the afternoon's quiet wealth,
how its serenade knits the various
ages of the day together,
the gleam of spider web clinging to the air
like a floating fibre of lung, a tightrope
of light between two porch posts, the dew
settling for the night on tomorrow's raw dawn.
These esoteric signs are everywhere
if signs they are, the future tropes
never guaranteed. Things might
contradict themselves, I hope.
Such simplicity is finite – the natural
bedfellows of harmony and discord.
That pebble in my shoe
will make itself eventually known.
Not everyone can say as much.

What We Saw in the Sky to the East

1. Kite

Remember. The past is gone for the moment.
Take hold of this string, its umbilicus of knots,
let your kite out slowly beyond the power lines
shaking off the starlings as you go.

Wait. There is nothing you can do. The wind
will not dry your shirts any faster if you
look away. The kettle will not boil, the custard
not set, the lava in your blood not cool.

Look. Here is my tea cup. There is your spoon.
The music of our little whirlpool.
My fork, your knife. Montague and Capulet.
Tintinnabulation of swords.

Give me shelter, or something, the lyrics of the old
songs go. Wipe the fever from my brow
with a handkerchief of cash. It's a false dichotomy
to think the sky belongs to any one of us.

Get out of the pool! the parrots cry in panic
at the coming storm. Clouds gather in doubt
like old scones, green with the gall of snow,
the chlorine catching at your throat.

Tempted? It won't take long to drink that glass of water.
Perhaps you'd like a straw, a desert to suck it up in
like a camel? Perhaps it won't even slake
your thirst. Perhaps only blood will.

Turn yourself inside out. That way we can see
whether or not you've eaten your greens. Not a pretty
sight, but like the violence of the big fish eating the little
fish, that's life, and at least someone is happy.

Consider. There on the street, an abandoned doll.
A doll with hair pulled out by the roots. One
eye missing. The last thing it saw plain in the expression
on its face. Perhaps not a doll at all. Perhaps a child.

In the china shop. Plates. Saucers. Gravy boats.
All that fine porcelain. The lathered bull,
banderillas dangling from his back, horns dripping,
weighing up his options. Who's next?

On my hot tin roof nine cats living one musical life:
a tortoiseshell, a tabby, a Persian, a Siamese,
a Sphinx, an Abyssinian, a Scottish Fold, a Liger,
a Manx without his rudder or, indeed, the attitude.

Here is a brick. Here another. Between them
a slice of cement like the filling in a cream biscuit
squeezed between the vertebrae. Another achievement
of age. In this fashion your tomb is well constructed.

2. Apple Cart

Hold everything. Are those tulips hatching? Grain
by grain the crumbs of earth tumble aside as the sun warms
its breakfast. Lie on your stomach, worm your way into it,
observe this enterprise until you too take root.

Feel this rose. It wants to be a magnolia,
or else an exotic brand name in a line of Super Model
Parfum: 'Badness' or 'Death.' The florist has warned it
against unrealistic ambition, to know its place in the posy.

Pause for rumination. Wipe your fingers
on your pants. Is that spinach or wisteria
between your teeth? Pray the mother-in-law
doesn't notice, you'll never hear the end of it.

Dilate your pupils by staring at the night.
The less you see the more you'll smell. Taste
this, it's deafening. Of all my senses the sense
of the ridiculous is my fave.

Look. I reserved a seat for you. Here's an apricot,
a chicken wing. Sit with me as the lions make
their entrance. The wilting giraffes. The pilgrims
on their knees. How can they sing at a time like this?

Count the bodies of the dead as they mount up
in the courtyard. This is what sells newspapers.
The autumn leaves crackle, the sibilant
broom hisses across the flagstones like hail.

Don't sit there. My scorpion has escaped. It's around
here somewhere. I've taught it how to curl its sting
and beckon like a prophet, but you never know, by
now someone else may have taught it how to point.

Who is he? Begging for alms again. Upsetting
the apple cart again. His mother inconsolable
squatting in the dust. Here is some milk. See
how it drips through the holes in his palms.

Remember, the future is a long time forgotten.
The starlings warm their claws on the humming wires.
Your kite out over the ocean, onward and upward,
its severed tail drifting over the houses.

Funny Hat

I met a man the other day
walking through the quiet streets
with a parrot on his head.

What's that on your head? I said
and he replied: A parrot.
What sort? I was genuinely curious.

An African Grey Parrot, and what's more
her name is Dorothy.
Remarkable, I said, for it goes without

saying that African Grey Parrots
are a rarity in my neighbourhood.
The parrot had leather vest and a little leash

to stop it flying off. As we paused
he placed the bird on the ground.
It waddled over to me

and implementing both beak and prehensile
claw it climbed up my trouser leg
like a monkey up a banana tree.

And how old is Dorothy? I asked
and he said: One hundred and seven years old.
Even more remarkable

for by now the nimble parrot had reached
my shoulder where it gripped my ear
like a biscuit in its beak and bit.

I cried out, but the intervention I sought
was not forthcoming. Instead
the man looked at me as if I were the one

interfering with his parrot.
The truth of my experience
as different from his

as a shadow from its host.
He plucked the bird rudely from my shoulder,
replaced it on his head, (he was wearing

a funny hat), wandering off
through the bright, dreamy, unknowable
light of an afternoon in our time.

Hand to Mouth

As a picture of modern urban poverty
it almost breaks your heart.
Old Mother Hubbard's bare boned cupboard,
her dog drooling optimistically.
What happened to Mr. Hubbard?
Down the pub most likely, drinking away the family savings;
run off with Mary Lou from the office
that short sighted gold digger. Or perhaps
he's dead from a coronary occlusion,
struck down by falling space junk.
Maybe it's the old man's bones
she's been feeding the dog all this time?
And what sort of dog is it? A corgi? A rottweiler?
Where are her children? Merchant bankers all.
What ever happened that dog ain't getting any fatter
what with the price of bones these days.
All these fruitless hypotheses.
It only remains to be said that in threadbare rags
Old Mother Hubbard doesn't have two sticks to rub together,
the dog next on the menu.

Interesting Times

I have lost the impetus to carry you
even though the apocalypse is hot
on our heels. Across the fields of broken
glass we waltz from one disaster
to the next in a vertigo of headlines.
Friendly fire – another name for motherhood
but don't let that put you off. Be born. Argue the toss,
dousing the future's prospectus
with tales of the glory days.
Remember when we used to breathe unassisted?
Extrapolate ambition to the realm of human reverie
which is where I do my best work.
I want to ask not *why*, not *how*, but *when*
will justice tumble from the sky?
now that each gavel has been reduced to ash,
every opinion freed of its carbon monoxide.
Give me one last séance – another chance
to expunge regret, or else flaunt it from the ramparts.
Count the cost of all that arrogance.
If it had not come to this
it would have surely come to something else.
What omens did we ignore back when we had prescience?
The future screaming in our faces like a crow on fire.
Using our children to stem the tide -
bon appetite my darlings, garnish your last
supper with franking credits, they'll taste
even better in the crematorium
of the natural world, enough to pay
for a sturdy, resilient, asbestos crypt
reinforced to withstand the blast

of your disdain. It's well deserved,
no one is denying that. I am merely
trying to find a final resting place in the shade
where I can enjoy my hoardings.
All I ever wanted was the opportunity
to re-train the young idiot I once was,
point him in the direction humanity
took at the crossroads.
Here, child, take my bones, grind them into bread.
I am the last person I expected
to meet on this side of the river, having paid
the ferryman in advance. Who is this doppelganger?
Glass half empty – bah humbug. *Amnesia* – remember
to wipe your feet on the welcome mat.
I will open gullibility's door
and inhale to the sponge of my lungs
the hot air of the oven. It surely couldn't happen here,
the raw ember of me as ambivalent
as right from wrong, I could barely tell
the difference in the tide pool of my swirling blood.
The whirling dervish of this longing
like a drill bit chowing down through steel.
The positive things I have done in my life
I could count on the fingers of one hand.
Beneath my feet the dormant
corms shrivel in their sleep,
needing flame to flower, while I dilly-
dally, squandering my time like an alchemist
who has tried to make something out of nothing,
only to realise nothing was better.
It's hard to keep a straight face in the face of all this smoke.
Wind from the south followed by wind
from the north. Trapped between, we crawl

along a narrow nave of bitumen.
The morning's irony of rain leaning down like a veil
will not be lost on the weather weary.
The trees shaking as wet dogs do
with relief from the heat.
Where did all this water come from?
Flame or ice or sarcasm?
It's all I can do to keep panic at bay,
to accept that life somehow includes us.
The silver spoon in my pants,
see where that has got me?
The lessons of bewilderment
lead through the ravaged forest
as though the smoke did not exist.
From the troubled edge of the scorched town, look,
the first petals of a tiny, blue-veined crocus.

Trees Without Passports

Between two palm trees thick with starlings
the horizon flattens the waves
beneath the sea's heavy rag.
Here before we were, the ocean runs downhill
from the perpendicular of one trunk to its partner.
Like me, the rough exterior keeping balloons
and children off with a thorny I-told-you-so.
Raffia fronds hang from the crowns
exhausted with salt and the natural way of age.
Who was here first, the apple or the cactus?
asks the non-stop chatter of the starlings.
Those roughed-up trunks frame only the view,
not a way of living in this world,
subsistence requires something more.
The direction of the swell
poised in anticipation of a photograph
aren't they same waves as yesterday?
One of these days the sea will kick a goal,
where the water in its never-ceasing movement,
examines, up close and personal, the new status quo.
Gulls will confuse themselves with pigeons
and why not? It's all confusing. Are those bananas
or sausages? That cold hand of death.
Unripe dates hang competing with the street lights,
orange and testicular like the ganglions
of pendulum clocks, still carrying on
an hour behind the dwindling sun.
We've lived here for many a year.
The view between the palm trees still
thick with starlings and their parasites,

they'll not put up much resistance
and who else will remember them?

In the Ladies Parlour — Woodford Academy

"Dreamt of a white baby with a strange head found in a basket of rubbish..."
— The diary of Jess McManamey

Whose dream was this beneath the unfamiliar stars?
Who are these twins in pinnies
poised for the camera like chess pieces?
Don't smile. Look ethereal.
This incarnation is only for a moment.

Fossicking in a sewing basket, amidst the threads
and thimbles, an old grooved bobbin
splitting with age like a gravid acorn.
What might this portend in the drawer shoved shut?

Is that music you hear?
Within this stone core, the parlour walls
once rang with muffled reels of the dancing diggers.
Magpie notes in F — flat carolling from the piano,
its arthritic keyboard dull as wooden teeth.

Don't open the curtain, outside someone might be hanging.

In the linen room — What's that? — It's naught
but a haunted footstep, squeaky apparition of a loose
floorboard. Think of gold and the ravenous dawn.
Think of us left behind in the journey's pause.
Whose strange-headed dream is this? Yours.

Look around you.
The luxuriantly moustachioed peer down
from the walls, the twins in pinafores,
vaguely familiar. Returning our gaze,
those strangers in the mirror.

Cogito Ergo Something

"Reader, I myself am the subject of my book: it is not reasonable you should
  employ your time on a topic so frivolous and so vain. Therefore, farewell."
  – Montaigne

I myself am the subject of my poem
against advice and contemporary fashion.
Here goes: I have 206 bones.
They are all inside.
My appetites are unexceptional apart from quantity.
I am of a certain height, the import
of which will aid only the coffin maker.
I own less hair than I did in the seventies when hair was utilitarian.
My weight is a sad situation.
Eighty percent of my brain is water.
My skin is the largest organ of my body and also the prettiest,
most of it is under my bed.
I am a lazy person except when I am doing something
I find interesting like walking the dog, or gazing at the sky,
or proving my existence, or demonstrating how a thing
and the word for a thing are different things.
How even a Prime Mover gets tired.
My ears and nose are still growing.
My blood type is O positive.
I think.
I get claustrophobic in traffic jams.
There is enough bacteria on my person to fill a soup can.
I have never taken Largactil
although my brother did, if that counts.
I watched his creeping ruin and did nothing
to halt that pale dissolution.
The word 'self' is an unknowable commodity

unless it is a stone.

I have most of my teeth.

My soul is the colour of sausages.

I look forward to my decrepitude, perhaps it's here already.

I am not the subject of my poem

dear reader, according to the experts

you are.

Talon

(I thought it lost
like a gate left open
or a one-winged parenthesis,
the hooked talon
my father brought back from India
in 1932, and later gave to me
when I was eight.
I blamed my brother
for not taking better care of it,
for leaving the gate open,
yet five decades later
when it re-emerged
amongst my mother's things
I recognised it instantly
like an old dream burst into life.
Nestled in a drawer
amongst tarnished coins and rings,
a substantial collection of dust,
I was amazed how memories
lie dormant in vivid sleep.
How long it took grief to fade
from the miscellany of emotions
How long it took to bury
with the other dead.
Close brackets.)

Hit Dog

There is a woman staggering in circles
on the front lawn. This happens moments
after the tyres squeal and a faint thump
interrupts the afternoon's quiet lassitude.

The woman has her hands to her mouth,
her jaw agape in nauseous shock.
'I've just hit a dog,' she says.
On the road a small grey twitching bundle.

I want to pat her on the back, calm her down,
but see there are other things to happen first.
The dog is breathing, then it stops. It's eyes glaze
over, staring at nothing. The woman sobs.

A man who has a pair of gardening gloves
lifts the dog off the road. The dog's shit is green.
We wrap an old towel around it.
More people come, a youth with tattoos.

The phone number on the tag on the collar
doesn't work. Then it does. Another man
who owns the dog comes running
from a nearby house still talking on the phone.

The look on his face awry with what storm
he knows is coming. New to the neighbourhood,
I didn't even know he owned a dog. He puts
his face to the dog's, an act too intimate for us.

There is palpable tension between the man
cradling his dead dog and the sobbing woman.
I say, 'That's the second time that's happened,'
but no one hears me. All the people stand about

helplessly: a scene from Brechtian theatre.
It's like the day has been stripped back
to its raw suburban elements. Then another
woman comes running from the neighbours

house, screaming and running, *'Are you sure?*
Are you sure?' They hold the bundle between
them and there is more screaming and sobbing.
Then the neighbours take away their dog

while we bring the shocked woman, who clearly
cannot drive, inside with us. Everyone else moves
off into the alarming clarity of the afternoon.
I say again, 'That's the second time that's happened.'

The 'Riff

       down the 'Riff I see Jen Maiden
perched on the roof of the Joan as if
she's about to take off like a honeyeater.
Below the concrete waits to catch her,
though her poems fly about like moths.
The Astroturf about as close to nature
as the pigeons can tolerate.
Even the passing embryos have tatts.
Everyone waiting for their car to be serviced.
The shadows of leaves float across
the ground like coins, bleached as coral
at the bottom of the plaza fountain.
Make a wish! Make a wish!
Here come the cops.
No one wants to be anywhere else.

Sound Track

Dancing like the dead
the leaves jump beneath the gurlet
blows of hailstones like Warren Beatty and Faye
Dunaway at the end of Bonnie & Clyde.
It might be stretching a point, and yet,
despite the thunder, the sky is still blue.

The machine-gunned villagers
in the black and white newsreel
are the silent witnesses now opposed
to the sun, the leaves' stains outlined on the path
steaming like the aftermath of fire.
Forthright in its silence

the road smokes like a tea break.
The survivors peek from beneath
the bodies of their fellows, playing
possum until, the tapping on the roof
subsiding, the sun revives
and the mood music changes.

Peach Tree

The peach tree beyond the fly-strewn window took years to declare itself. Reason being the gouged trunk full of rot, spreading year by year, up the trunk and out the lateral branches, spilling sawdust like a punctured doll. Half the year it looked dead. How long have I looked at it before thinking this? I considered chopping the whole thing down, planting another, but each year as the rot spread, blossom erupted like a snowstorm vivid in fistfuls of unthrown confetti. Some final blooming a few days a year before the winds laid waste and birds returned to feast, comparing last year's scarred harvest to this. I feel lucky with what chance has left, a few days flowering, the sudden profit of staying in one place a long time. The punier the fruit the more blessed the flower.

My Ears

I was born with my ears on backwards. That is to say the conventional disposition of ears, in my case, was reversed. Namely, the left ear is on the right side of my head and the right ear has ended up correspondingly on the left. As a consequence, my ears face backwards. Otherwise, my head is quite symmetrical. Due to the sonic vibrations of the shell-like audio conduits, I hear backwards. Backwards hear I. No one ever sneaks up on me. I am good at overhearing conversations going on behind my back. The whisper of gossip nothing new. Unfortunately, I'm not so good at negotiating busy intersections where the noise in front of me, voices for instance, traffic, seems to come from everywhere at once. They tell me there is a surgical procedure that will rectify this condition, but I don't know. It's the way I was born. I have tried walking backwards and there is some merit in that strategy, albeit to the detriment of my vision. A mirror helps. I'm not so much interested in what lies ahead. Only that I have to be careful. I'm more interested in the passing echo of where I have been, the lesson long learned, the echo passing of who once I was.

Rat Nest

Responding to the screams I found her holding up a bundle of rags secreted behind the paint tins. Her face white with ordinary horror, as blind baby rodents tumbled from the ransacked nest. They were in her hair, clinging to her arms, the ragball aloft above her head. Clearly poison had not worked. I bundled them all into a water-filled bucket stirred and stirred until the only movement was the little whirlpool swirling to stillness. She washed her hair compulsively. Cleaned. Washed. Cleaned again. That night the she-rat scrambled through the walls and cupboards, searching, squealing, frantically scratching until, at last, it stood on its haunches in a corner of my nightmare, twitching at me, unafraid.

The Hippos of Venezuela

Poor old Pablo Escobar,
sad, misunderstood fellow.
Once the Florida beach has been emptied
of all that Columbian marching powder,
dispersed like a burst apiary across the flatlands
of an insatiable market, there is still the problem
of what to do about the cash.
The submarine, commandeered from the navy,
is too small. They have to leave pallets of cold hard
greenbacks on the beach like bales of hay after harvest
or turtles returning to the sea.
That irks.
You'd think that when there is more money
than will fit in a submarine then money might
lose something of its meaning. Not on your life.
What to spend it on? That is the question.
Of course, if you're Pablo Escobar, you might
decide to fix the nation's hospital system or instead,
warned off politics, you might buy your own private zoo,
fill it with exotic creatures from all over the known
world. You might even call it philanthropy.
However, when you tread on too many toes
and get yourself shot, for one – who cares?
and for two - who's going to look after the poor animals?
Not the cartel henchmen sick of stirring corpses
into vats of acid, worthy work though that might be.
The bars inevitably rust, the palm trees fall over,
the cheap concrete decays.
Hunger drives the captive animals to do what captives do
and break out, so now the hippopotami, rampaging

through the compound, muddy after the monsoons,
have long escaped not only into the *Meta* and *Vichada*,
but also the *Venturai*, the *Orinoco*, the *Avauca* rivers.
Another ecological disaster.
Like submarines the hippopotami don't stop
for national borders; it's their perfect environment,
all the wide wandering *Amazon* before them.
Poor old Pablo Escobar, coked off his scone
at the centre of the universe, invincible
behind those bullet-proof bales of cash —
when you try to play God in a Godless world,
God shoots back.

Ann Hodges, 1954

— only person known to have been struck by a meteor

Sheesh,
talk about wrong place at the wrong time.
Out watering the petunias on a golden summer's
evening, when out of a clear sky...
That glancing, blackened bruise on her hip
like a shark's taken a bite out of her
and disliked the taste.
On the other hand an inch or two
to the left and she'd be a goner.
Space dust. She picks herself up.
Could've made a mozza
on the live chat show circuit,
but given it's the fifties
and colour tv's only just been invented
there's probably hoovering to be done.
The mess that meteor's made of the front
yard, on its way to one in a billion.
Poor Ann. Just her luck.
Alien germs all over her.
Scrubbed down in the radiation tent.
Ruined a good dress too.

Communion of Stones

The nearly full moon rises swiftly over the silhouette
        of Narrowneck plateau,
its light cast above the sodden valley paddocks.
        I want to detach myself from my shadow
and pace out its sudden length as it falls across
        the grass, vivid as daylight.

Dogs lounge coiled by the fire,
        we admire them, in our skin, in our bones.
Ducks hiss and conspire with the dam. Amongst other things
        the night lists its fears, itemized, rescinded.
A communion of stones cracks in the glowing heat of the pit.
        The aqueous humour boils in my eye.

Against the night sky four shooting stars
        pace the frailty of this slow wheeling.

Shackleton's Hut

"The inside of the hut was not long in being fully furnished and a great change
it was from the bare shell of our first days of occupancy."
— Ernest Shackleton, 1908

Within the wooden hut the frozen ghosts remain.
The spectre of each image lurks in the memory
of a shadow, behind a door, just out of sight.
Consider these populated silences.
Not even dust settles among the socks,
which might be granite socks, hanging year
after year as though pegged in a catacomb.

The cupboards, made of packing crates, hold nothing more
than the chill of gleeful abandonment.
Not an insect stirs, nor interrupts.
Examine if you will the mausoleum of the bunks
their cold blankets like the hides of strange carcasses.
An icy hawser entwined about itself, the slowly growing
greying whiskers of the rope, left alone these hundred
years like a Grandmother's fossilised plait,
unmoved from where the last hand dropped it.

Beyond the stony beach the waves freeze mid
splash, the cliffs like bitten coconut,
and in the distance, sounding like a crepitating
gin & tonic in a long glass,
the Big Pav.
We are more concerned for the minutiae of wood,
the planks clinging to their weeping nails.
Even a gnarled crucifix with its bunions and knots,

wired to a shivering rock, is barely enough to divide
the ocean from the sky.
Not a single person but for his echo.

Dirty ice they call this melting slush,
or is it the slowly freezing sheet of sea
cohering to its own repetition.
Brr, that water looks cold.
Look at that microcosm's patch of snow,
those nail holes stopped in time, or else the peppered
expanse from east to west across the bare horizon
where no rescue comes galloping.

Where did the timbers come from that built this hut
to keep the emptiness at bay?
Who cooked? Who swept the floors?
From a wire line a pair of torn pants still hangs as though
waiting for their owner to return with a darning needle.
The axe marks in the boards where once a walrus,
sundered for the evening stew, bled out.
What might have been that vision
drowned in hunger and sorrow?
A butcher with an axe and a job to do.
                    Oh the whisky, the poor whisky
                    lost at the bottom of the iced-over sea.

On the distant side of Pony Lake the muttering penguins
stand about like onlookers at an accident,
perhaps the sinking of a ship through ice,
waiting for the cops to move them on.
In leaning light the tinned stuff of survival sits
rusted to the shelves, ephemeral and eternal as one.

Everywhere you look:

> *Irish Brawn,*
> *W. P. Hartley's Red Plum*
> *Bottled Pickles Liquid*
> *Aberdeen Marrow Fat,*
> *Sweet Midget Gherkins*
> *Moir's Red Currants,*
> *Fry's Concentrated Cocoa*
> *Henry Tate & Sons Sugar Cubes*
> *Toothpowder Entirely Free From Injurious Acids.*

A hot meal every evening,
the fire not permitted to go out.
All the makeshift shelving, neat
and tidy against the nightly blizzard's onslaught.
Also:
reams of mouldering paper for the first Antarctic novel.
Why else bring the printing press,
rich with jettisoned metaphor?
Bamboo snow shoes for the ponies,
like coiled hotplates on the Columbian stove.
The freshly washed braid of a fraying cable.
Man's best friend, otherwise known
as his hot water bottle, hanging on the back of a warped
door, while outside, still tethered to its stake
beside the empty kennels, white and scoured as ivory,
one of the dogs gives up its ribs to the wind.

Each shadow a frozen moment,
not even death has thawed them out,
those specimens mummified with cold.
Count them: 24 porcelain insulators –
like a string of teeth around a cannibal's neck.
Crystal spheres of pipettes in the lab

busy with fairies of ice, a chemical residue
in each, a dream's spark imagined
in apprehended bubbles of flight.

A chair wrapped in Hessian sacking to keep its shoulders warm.
The twisted mess of the first bicycle too fragile for its mission.
A petrified shaving brush for those who recall the empire.
King Edward and his Queen still hanging from a wall,
the toasts ever-ringing in the air with the clink of metal mugs.
> *Oh the whisky, the poor whisky*
> *lost at the bottom of the cold cold sea.*

Look: a roll of gauze bandage, itself a sepia wound.
Coiled serpent of the enema bag.
A patch of mould on a canvas tarpaulin
like the fur of a dead marsupial.
A box of broken eggs. A pair
of copper-ringed cuff-links like simultaneous sides of the moon.
Who'd need cuff-links in a place like this?
The leopard spots of rust on a shovel's silent face.
The loneliness of a safety pin.
Everywhere you look
each window an oblique glimpse of light
devoid of conversation.
Outside the great sugared continent
stretching away as far as it is possible to go
in time and distance on ski or sled, impossible to trace
from these frail maps, the wind howling across
the twisting canyons in the sea,
the moulins running with ice water
pattern of their own design.

Building Site

I've done my dash of labouring. All the heavy lifting's paid
my young man's dues and left me wanting. Like art, its message
behind a portable steel fence is: *Keep out, construction site.*
I've lost the credentials, apart from splinters and lesions.
The sunspots evidence of too much time in the midday glare,
mixing mud in a barrow, too long away from my pina colada.

Don't miss the cacophony of jackhammers and circular saws.
The making of something useful where nothing was before,
but do I admire it more than the building of something
useless? Sure, I used to lug a bag of cement over my shoulder,
like a rescued grandma from a burning tower as well as any
fireman. Sadly, no more. The fence says: *Do not enter. Back off.*

I can flatten my vowels, imitate the discourse but it's been
too long. Those tradies understand I'm an imposter. I might know
an adze from an awl, a plane from a bar, but they know I'm a fake —
which the nail punch? which the banjo? In my human cloak
of age I can hit my thumb with a hammer along with the best of
them, scream to the high heavens, tear the whole sandcastle down.

Monotreme

He must have been tired
six days out from Sydney town,
       having been shown some ancient
cataracts and arable pastureland
dormant beneath primitive sclerophyll forest.

Having accounted for Hobart's intricate grace
from the top of Mt Wellington –
       rising sea levels seemed to say it all,
now how do I get down? The guide didn't know.
They traipsed about, lost, for several hours.

He'd been away from home a long time,
missing the comfort of his bed, perhaps.
       Banks was right, plenty of Banksias.
Somewhere along the track to Bathurst
someone produced a curious creature

the excellent flat-footed, duck-bill platypus
with its poisonous spur and habit of laying eggs.
       What place might such a being
have in his new schema of regarding the world?
He must have been tired

for as records fail to show
Darwin gave a little shrug, a stifled yawn
       as he handed the creature back, not curious, no.
Nor quite ready to yield up God, despite
God, hereabouts, being nowhere to be seen.

Silvereyes

Startled, the little Silvereyes
dash to the heart of the drought bush
protected by its brittle armoury of thorns.
One by one, like falling autumn
they drop to the straw coloured grass
recommence their foraging.
Startled again, my shoe scraping
on gravel, the passing shadow of a crow
they flee once more to the centre
co-ordinated as one breathing thing.
One by two, like mice with wings
(and silver eyes) the tiny birds
float to the ground, repeat, float
like autumn, repeat, float, repeat again.

Ibis

The reviled and opportunistic sacred ibis
strolls the lawns of the botanical gardens
like a casual flaneur hoping for crusts.
The trouble is it looks so ungrateful
as if all the crusts and scraps belong
to it alone, with its curved beak
manufactured like a surgical calliper,
perfectly evolved for sifting bins.
Indifferent to the loathing heaped
upon its scabrous head it languishes
in the same lowly category of disgust
as the rat, the gull, the flying fox the guano
of which is turning the garden to a wasteland.
Perhaps it is not the ibis, but we
whom hubris infects, wanting
to dictate who may pick, who deserves.
Like so many, we want the ibis to look
humbler, to abject itself before the charity
of our perfectly evolved disdain.

Turtle

Like a couple of dirty dinner plates
an eastern long-necked turtle
waddles across the road as though
straining its chin for the winning post.
The topography of its shell describes
new ways of mapping the world.
Cars divert around and over, stopping
to let it inch a few steps forward
lifting its feet as if the road
is too hot, the stones at the shoulder
too sharp. When I stop, it stops.
Moves when I move. In time it will make
the pond on the far side, slide beneath
the surface like a hubcap filling with water.

On the Shoalhaven

"Art doesn't alter things. It points things out, but it doesn't alter them."
– Arthur Boyd

Across the lacquered varnish
of the river, rain comes dimpling
the surface with a sibilant hiss
like the sound of fat sizzling.

Old boulders have come down
hill to examine their own unshaven
reflections in the mirror, come down
from the places they left a millennium

ago, a moment in the ongoing stillness
of boulders. Other rocks have also
escaped their portraits. In contrast
the fleeting water follows

its memory embedded in the river.
The life of shifting sand,
submerged tree trunks which never
stay still for long, these turn and

lean to the current's bidding, all
with a singular purpose. This far
upstream where salt water stalls
and dilutes itself with air,

small whirlpools play about
the snags beneath. The broken
illusion of tranquility merging to the right
like a long, sweeping brush stroke

gliding to its vanishing point
where rare stuttering frogs read the news
to each other, and the water's faint
gossip around the bend continues

on beneath a distant bridge. Soon it will
dissolve with time, nudging downstream
to the coast. Too late for the speed
boats who, tomorrow, will return

and cross the river Styx like a rip
down the centre of the canvas, stitched
up with mud and melting spit
giving form to a great amnesia.

The ripples will soon subside,
the boulders quietly exhale
as the river accepts the inward tide
of a world reverting to scale.

Ludmilla's Cottage

In the valley mist curdles
about the wood pile's limbs,
an axe handle lying across them like a tusk
cold with more than dawn.

Bereft of his bones Otto's shirt
clings to the line by its wrists,
rheumatic with frost,
finger nails of dew frozen to the rope.
The illusion of a man about the place.

Both the same temperature the moon and the sun
overtake each other, going their separate ways.
The moon's lichen staining the cracked surface
of its dish. Behind skeins of rapid cloud
a blinking bulb with broken filament.

In the hut an unsteady table
(wedge of cardboard beneath the wonky leg
lost for the moment).
On the table a wooden bowl split down the grain,
and in the bowl a pile of sucked cherry stones,
withered stems like a fallen orchard.

Beneath the bark shingles
each cupboard door a different shade of lemon,
the flaking paint of dripping flags.
The paint tins glued shut.
Otto's boots at ease, their tongues swollen with thirst.

In her ice chest a jar of blackberry jam
cellophane lid held on with a rubber band.
A rock of cheese that might be soap.
A flaccid carrot. Still enough milk
in the bottom of the carton.
The empty shelves of tomorrow's list.

On the window sill a paper boat
folded in the Japanese style
filled with loose change
and a shrunken mandarin.

The road through the evening forest
like a whitened scar. Gravel
like honeycomb, the drive much longer now,
the red eyes of roos in the headlights
slowing her down.

Beneath the pillow his old beanie
threads of wool coming loose
after all this time frayed with silverfish.

The Chorus Girl

1.
Inside this box of old photos
she is wrapped in a dead bear.
The shallow day receding
where the river takes a gradual turn to the left.
It might be the Yarra but for the snow
slapped on one side of the tree trunks.

2.
And here are her wrists, supporting her chin. The hair
style circa 1930's bob. Those theatrical teeth to die for.
Cowled by pines and a three o'clock shadow of rhododendrons.
We are trying to make sense of one another.
Who, for instance, is this Great Man beside her?
What a fine looking specimen, in round spectacles
and a white bow tie. Give such a man
a white bow tie and a tyrant is born.

3.
Let us neglect no landmarks.
Here is the famous Banbury cross.
She so small at the foot of the spire
in the middle of the road.
Queen Victoria, or perhaps it is the Mother of God
looking as if she is about to ash a cigar
on her head.

4.

The tiny shoulder-bag hanging at her waist; eyes beneath hat brim.
The angle of its shadow, like a caul, tells me it is late morning.
She is perched on the top fence railing looking
as though she is about to topple into the canna lilies.
Her hand raised in a rhetorical gesture. *Mosquito*
hunting in the wild west. I was going to strike a lovely pose
but the damn skeeter butted in just as it was snapped.
The strength in her arm a fascist salute
about to give emphasis to an asterisk of blood.

5.

She and a friend rehearsing backstage
(scenery painted on an overexposed bedsheet).
She is dancing. Her partner in a Marie Antoinette wig
with lots of flounce and icing frill.
Symbiotic fingers entwined.
She is wearing doublet and hose,
jacket and clogs, toes perfectly pointed
like the hands of a stopped clock.
Being the taller, she is the man.

6.

Theatrical Company viewing printing presses, 9/3/1933.
There are 32 of them. A handsome group. 16 men and 16 women.
Gruda, Lance, Etsie, Tommy, Beatie, Julian, Gigi, Freddie
and the others standing before great reams of paper, a metropolis
of pipes and strange machinery. Each one of them holds tomorrow's
paper. Perhaps after an opening night of champagne
and cigarillos, the whole company in suits and furs
have raced to the printing presses to see the first notices
roll off the belt and cool on the printery floor.
Which one is *Herr Direktor?*

Where is his white bow tie?
Every one looks like they have been cut
from another photograph and stuck before this bizarre
backdrop of the presses. She smells of dust. It is deepest night.

7.

Travelling in the tropics.
Shorts and sandals, picking coconuts
from a dwarf coconut palm,
unless they are paw-paws.
Behind her, fishbone ferns
camouflaging a cardboard oasis.
Her happiness, her happiness.

8.

Out of focus. Hand on hip,
a deliberate pose in tweed civilian skirt.
Behind her, across the courtyard
the black and white stained glass windows,
the ivy swathed fenestra of the grand archway.
What don took this snap? Such an image
suggests that hers was not a long stay at Oxford.
Tyre marks in the gravel arc past
as if she has been brushed by a skidding comet.

9.

Fifteen ladies at a country cricket match.
It is difficult to work out the pencilled names on the back.
The pose is natural, legs crossed under her,
giving weight to one wrist. In this happy snap
every one of these ladies is wearing a magnificent hat.

10.
Back in Australia. Groongal.
Verandah, early morning light.
Don't I look clean? she has written on the back,
flapping a sheet's ghost in the sun.

11.
-YNGRING is all that can be read of the railway station sign.
Ballast and shadows.
On tour, presumably.
Great levers of the rail siding with its still life of pigeons.
She is sitting in a wheelbarrow amongst her girlfriends
waiting for a train. Who is missing from this photo?
Who is the gossip about?

12.
Sitting on the middle rung of yet another railing fence
at the edge of the bush. In white shorts,
her legs hang down in weeds and thistles, a background
of eucalypts tells us we are somewhere familiar, but where?
The wild and undeveloped nature of the scene,
the spirit level of the horizon on her shoulders.
Her finger rests on the parallel strand of the top wire,
as if it was a cello string about to be plucked.
She is young. This is home.

13.
Holding out her wings like an emperor butterfly.
A dress as wide as she is tall. Look at those hoops,
those daring shoulders The armlet at her bicep is not flattering,
squeezing a bulge of fat up into her underarm.
But she is smiling, as is the recent fashion,
and a wedge of optimistic sunshine

is coming through the skylight of the rehearsal shed roof.
Something beyond the ordinary
process of photographic development
has tinkered with the negative
so that a poltergeist's fingers
are about to seize her from behind.
That distorted shadow is a giant fish
and she is in its mouth.

14.
Here she is outside the stage door.
Is she the peasant girl in Rumplestiltskin?
Mary Pickford curls hang down from her bonnet.
She is spinning wool, or rather spinning hair
into gold. Probably it is nothing more than the threads
of an old doormat. All is illusion. Spinning wheel
too shiny and black, fresh from the props department.
Her waist contained by a gypsy's corset.
If she wears shoes they must be red. Wild peasant girl
who will charm the modest hero in a rags to riches matinee
through the strange alchemy of that clot of human hair.

15.
There are 37 sepia people assembled for the curtain call
including several children and a large costumed cat.
A panto, by the looks of it. The background forest
has been so meticulously constructed the very shears
of Leonardo might have been set to scissoring work.
I cannot pick her from the crowd, though I am sure she is here.
A spear-carrier, perhaps. Or the cat.
Flat as a hieroglyph
she has disappeared inside her character.

16.

A haunting shot of her on a park bench at the side of a gravel path.
She has a book, or a box of chocolates, it is hard to tell on her lap.
She is wearing leather gloves. The bench is at the foot of an oak tree.
Several of its lower limbs have been lopped.
It has no leaves. Autumn, then.
A long way from home and death,
though these images all add up to the same thing.
The scene might have been desolate
but for the temptation of a smile
which could be a chocolate forever in her cheek.
Beyond this frame she dies alone.
In the leaves the fleeting sunlight is its own stone moment.

Soapbox Orator

1.

> Stinking of piss
in a hovel in Scotsdale
he slams the door
on the backs of Mormons
after lecturing them to numbness
on the follies of mammon.
Over the back paddock
he sees Mrs Christ come waddling
with his bucket of soup.
All about her head the moon
as night prepares for frost.

2.

> From Hyde Park to the Domain
he mounted his soap box
to denunciate God and politics,
to end up here in hermitude,
promulgating fairy tales, elves,
the comfort of leprechauns.
Where ever they fed him he spoke.
Ranted, some called it.
Caught frothing at the mouth
in black&white by *4 Corners*,
a hairy relic of yesteryear
in feverish oration.
No topic above contempt,
deserving of his wild rhetoric.
For six months a guest
of the Shah of Iran who

bade him peel grapes disguised
as proverbs and cinquains.
The Communists outstunted him.
Every dwarfed issue of the day.
Even your soft pop-star
in search of an answer
beguiled to convert to Islam,
who then renounced that crack
pot novelist. All the fuss
that followed. He slid back
up the spiral of his shell
appalled at the power
of grunting.

3.

      He turns his hearing aid
down to a murmur here in Scotsdale;
body language sufficient
human contact for anyone.
Childlessness his one saving grace.
Bark if you want his attention.
Throw things if there is smoke.
Yap, gesticulate, let your teeth
snap at his awful white neck
if you suspect he is alive beneath
the soup stains and all else
that he has been.
He will find the fire exit
alone, or else worm
his own warmth from the flames.

4.

       Outside, as frost settles
on shivering sheep,
old adversaries wake. Our
Mythical Lady, whom he loves
beyond logic, approaches
over the moonlit paddock.
Her dear deaf silence.
Her beautiful mute blue.
The offered caul
dripping in her hands
with the stars of her son's blood.

In Case of Fire

(i.m. Deb Westbury, 2018)

Rain skates
across the roof tops
blackening tiles, numb to all the predictions of rain. It offers universal
foil to dignity, ruffled feathers, wedding hats, washing weeping
into the thin space between chimney and clothes horse drying by the fire.

In the corner
a cardboard box
and in the box, wrapped in a shamrock tea towel a scorched baby possum
fallen down the chimney into the squealing flames. Next night and the next,
the mother possum returned, screeching down the chimney's hot throat.
The vet said it would not survive, but it did. Everyone else goes on.
Only you don't.

Walking home
from your house
I saw more uncollected species of birds than I have ever seen before.
All those parrots in their feathered trousers, the dusk that follows every bird
to its mystery, the ambush of each footstep like a street sign pointing two ways.
It might have been the wine, it might have been the grief welling behind
a future hour, that is, drop by drop, filling this room to the cornices.

The dust
of your voice
on my answering machine, a message received too late. Your phobia
comprehended; I don't think it has a name beyond *suffering*, manifest
in refusal to answer the phone. Nothing good ever comes of it. Bad news
crouches in your ear and will not leave.

Rain will not
douse the past.
Before you wake first you must drown. Only once I saw you struggle
through the bush. It was the tiny florets held your interest, not the grand
scale of the path, dimension of the journey back – that was for symbolists
and wankers. I asked once if you liked music and you said: 'Fuck no.'

The piano
in the corner
silent against the inside wall of the lounge room, clunking, you claimed,
as if being abused by a primary school teacher. I never heard you play.
So much of your life left to wayward imagination. It might have been different.
It might not have been different. It might have been worse.

It was. It is.
You are.
I know some of the houses where you lived, one in mournful earshot
of a donkey. The mutual understanding you had with the koori boys who'd
steal your car, and from whose house around the corner you'd steal back,
leave them a bottle of beer for looking after it. A little splosh.
The dearth of kindness in the world.

Here are the ashes
of your son
in an urn on the mantelpiece, beside your bed, where ever you are.
When the fires came I packed my books and important documents
necessary to explain my identity, a few clean clothes, photos, a toothbrush –
car of random possessions if and when the order came to flee.
Mother of these ashes, you packed your urn.

The skeleton

of a leaf

will do as a book mark. The bisected nautilus, plumes of coral and collected

South Coast shells adorning the bathroom window sill, an archipelago

of biography. Each one the story of its place in your life.

Then the rain.

Furniture Music

"We didn't eat every day, but we never missed an aperitif."
— J.P. Contamine de Latour, of his friendship with Erik Satie

One
or two
notes trickle
their way down the keyboard's haunted stairwell.
Eighty-four broken promises
to the one who is gone
secluding themselves
into a refrain.

One
or two notes
as if
creeping across the scales of a centipede,
the greased links of a bicycle chain
turning on its own oiled orbit,
trippingly
a cat stalking the piano's yellow ribs
developing a trope perhaps,
a theme, if not of flying giraffes
or some other *surrealisme*
then of loss   loss   loss.

        Play this piece without staves, he says.
        Play these notes as though limping.
She
sings in the tenements
where open windows look out
onto a broom swept square,

the doves
cooing for their recompense of crumbs,
mating for life and for the loss   loss
loss   of one imperfect love.
You.
She.
Second and third person subsumed
leaving the ragged imposture of the first.
Twirling on the circus trapeze like a fish.
You and the vertigo of you.
How can she contain such clumsy multitudes?
Yet yes, she does, you do.

In the cobblestone laneways he is bereft,
the alleyways through which she disappeared,
even though he calls, cries, cajoles
and curses.
His lost words in pursuit around a corner
to the empty square filled with flaneurs
those naked *gymnopedies,*
heels clicking
across the cobblestones like typewriters.
Amongst them, like a dove
with a cork foot,
she is nowhere to be found.
Nowhere call the carillon's bells, drifting down
from the egg shells of the Montmartre hills,
the clouds puffing out their varicose cheeks.
Gone.
In the time it takes
for an echo to choke in the river fog,
for a harsh word to set in its own aspic
the world recoils

from the soft decibels of loss   loss.

Lost
in his hovel
in *Arcueil*
seven grey suits hang from the ceiling.
Also, one hundred found umbrellas
like swans mummified in pitch,
plus eighty-four perfumed handkerchiefs.

Day by day he walks the stinking streets
of Paris without embellishment
in his grey, corduroy suits.
The velvet gentleman
with a liver made of moss
scourges his skin
with the dry pumice stone of his bath.
The music of armchairs
hypnotic and melancholy
like the streets devoid of her, she, me.
Every note he writes reaches through the fog.
The desolation of empty spaces,
the music of crossing from one doorway to another,
knocking, knocking, asking, searching,
never resting,
only, like a mouth the doorways remain forever
closed.

        Play this piece with one lung.
        Play this passage as though a ghost.
Do not call on him at home in *Arcueil*,
nor ask why he eats only food that is white
(but for the exception of green wormwood,

or the yellow of an omelette
made from the souls of thirty eggs).
You are not invited into this church of one.

When the time came to finally enter his hovel,
they found, apart from one hundred
waterproof swans wrapped in tar,
a scene described as one of indescribable squalor.
And
in addition
the unsent letters addressed to her.
She.
Suzanne.
Who is gone.
Unsent letters of thirty years,
describing
in no uncertain terms,
the broken armchairs of his life
decorated in the lilting notes,
of passing upholstery,
of never sitting,
of searching, always searching
the discord of this vast
and empty
city.

Suitcase

What can I say to you that isn't already a podcast?
Two-and-a-half hours on the road with lunch
in Wangaratta is hardly a life worth living.
All the cheese has melted like the ice caps.
Lava might be no worse. I swear to God this prayer
is no better than a yap flying by on the wind.
The rubbish bin is full of dead and injured magpies.
I saw the man who put them there running away.
My clothes are incongruous
with the general philosophy of the times.
The policeman did not find the drugs
you had stashed in your underpants
and from that moment your life was different.
Abstractions have too much influence.
My brothers once saw my identical twin
at the beach even though to my knowledge I have no twin.
I love your left profile more than your right,
your mug shot more than your happy family snap.
It's got something to do with the ears.
I wanted to believe you but thought, why bother?
Is that me at the bottom of your suitcase
or someone else?
Where are you taking us?

More Rhetorical Questions

How will we know what to ask
when all the sparrows have been silenced?

Who will open the crypts
when the last stones have been carved?

Where in the haystack is the truth's needle?
When will the dog have its day?

Who will take us to task in our squandering?
Why not bite the hand that feeds you?

Is sink or swim the only choice we get?

Why should we offer our throats
in either sacrifice or homage?

What would a saved earth look like,
begging in its rancorous rags?

Lines for Lyres

"If you are squeamish do not prod the beach rubble."
– Sappho

It begins with remembering to get some more milk,
    marching to the corner, coins jingling in your pocket.
One of these days you'll get to the end
    of the page and nothing will happen.
Each line accruing like sediment over the sunken
    bones at the bottom of a pond,
like the life of human history, the glue on a postage stamp
    atop the telecommunications tower,
the axolotl in the mud wondering what all the fuss is about.
    Long ago, O Best Beloved, ambition festered
in the primordial soup, followed by the nightmares
    of tooth and fang and fiscal collapse.
Watch the Futures market take a nose dive
    from the high point of modernism
to the low point of here and now.
    The next line lifts up its skirts
and scampers for the parochial hills, hellhounds
    hot on its tail. What's good for the goose
is grouse for the mouse, and righteousness
    assumes an authority that leaves a sour taste.
Not even an elephant will remember the milk of human apathy.
    Turn the page. Hold your breath.
When the archangels screech my name from the perch
    of the steps, watch me blow the rusty old trumpet
of my blunderbuss. The crows will drop
    from the sleeves of their cassocks and make short
work of the milk bottle tops left too long in the sun
    in any quadrangle, any weekday you care to name.

On the asphalt tarmac they peck the crumbs
of reason as if they were crumbs of something else.
All the birds queued up along the power lines like juries.
A dead sparrow full of heroin whacked over the razor wire,
that's how ingenuity operates in my neighbourhood.
The next line will leave itself open to misinterpretation,
the ace of clubs really my aorta cramping,
a metaphor for something, friend, though what?
The higher I climb the more I disappear,
the missing rungs of my ascent like holes in the ice,
like stanza breaks punctuating the Weddell Sea.
All those 60's sitcoms that shaped the parameters
of my youth, Gilligan, Captain Parmenter, Zeus
exerting their blind influence like gravity.
The bunny-rug of comfort is nothing more
than a burning flag tucked up to my chinny chin
chin. Are those flames art? Look closely,
you can see the Seurat in Laura Ashley;
listen and you'll hear the Stravinsky in Zappa, his beard
vast as a sun flare lying on the palliative
gurney, mirror image of eventually everyone. The guitars distort
like static and the unarmed audience prepares to riot.
Now I make elephant lists of disconsolate
things, including the spilt milk I am weeping over.
Other critical masses: cuff links I have worn,
lines uttered too soon or not at all,
old loves long gone like the flesh from a fossil.
Listen: the summer buzz of lawn mowers
coughing out territory and ownership.
I am adding my din to the general cacophony,
the dwarf songlines of my picket-fenced suburb —

don't blink or you'll miss them – stopping, as they do,
where the highway crosses the contaminated river
 and we proceed no further.
Hold your breath. Here come the new contagions.
 My main mode of perambulation these days
is the towpath of habit. Take
 a line, any line, stretch it as far as the raw foreskin of possibility will allow.
Not far. It's pretty limited.
 Where there is a rule there is a rebel.
Doubt is always a passenger in this sci-fi
 adventure, stay tuned for the future, (Rpt).
Dig a little deeper
 if you want to reach Nirvana. It's down
there somewhere. Suspension of disbelief is a luxury
 we can't afford in this political argy-bargy:
believe in everything, believe in nothing,
 your choice. The relations of the horse-fly
to the horse are less symbiotic than you might think,
 as are the cracks of the cow hide to the hip pocket nerve.
Please, please, disenfranchise me from your discourse
 and I'll disenfranchise you from mine.
Get your people to talk to my people
 in the grunts and semaphore they excel at.
As Wordsworth is to daffodils so am I to shame.
 All the ducks dead in the swamp,
no happy hunting ground, no exegesis.
 What happens when the world just fills up? What then?
Something from nothing is good advice, a soul
 from a test tube perhaps. Those syrupy bubbles percolating
to the surface of my latte, words are the froth
 around my lips, osculating the way a dragonfly

greets its own reflection in a pond.

Once I looked back on my future from a position of satiety.

Every traffic light caught my attention.

Each rose I might have stopped at.

All the thwarted orchids wanting more of my time.

The soup in the gravy boat won't make

regret any more palatable, if it's gravy

you want then look in my pocket. Examine the eastern

sky, the clouds gathering like oracles,

there's a prediction waiting to happen.

Much of the time I think I am taking notice

then comes the final exam at the end of term

and I realise I am not wearing any pants, my

blood has diluted and my thoughts have become yours.

Afterwards they came and pruned the saplings

of my youth but I forgot to ask for the sawdust.

If I had taken more risks with the lexicon then maybe

I might not have forgotten the end

of the sentence I was so desperately struggling to...

The past is nothing but a Nobel Prize ago,

a wasp sailing its way through a picnic.

Beneath the silt I am becoming stone.

In that epoch elbow grease was invented,

our two civilisations diverged, and the economy

of quid pro quo, eye for an eye, gained traction.

Our tired old houses were never so neat.

That moat you are digging in the ocean

already awash with stink. Hold your breath.

When I floated there I extolled the virtues of wanton sloth,

one of several sins at my disposal.

Most of the time I did not know what I was doing

and that would appear to be the point.
I am a stanza break in the Weddell Sea.

    The best part of the waking day – going back
to sleep, and when you get there all is ruin.

    Can you recall those lines we recited
to test the measure of our limbo?

    The hierarchy of terror in the playground,
the curdled milk ready for dissemination.

    In the economy of mammals the supermarket
chain has usurped the corner milk-bar,

    the cows all closed until further notice.
Take heed, O Best Beloved.

The Light Fantastic

Like sparks erupting from the campfire
when a new log of logic is thrown
on, a small galaxy, dense as frogspawn,
spirals up toward a smoky
corner of the universe.
Stop. No. The universe – really? Ex-
trapolated from a camp fire?

We sit around the perimeter
of the narrative toasting our Americanisms,
skipping to the end before the miasma
of night creeps upon us,
along with everything else
that lurks in the swamp.
Soon we will be roasting our children.

Staring into the embers we are blinded
by the possibilities of light,
eyes put out by over confidence
in our own abilities.
The shadow-puppets of flames
predicting civilisation and its downfall.
It only takes one errant star's decision

not to follow the crowd and all human
intellect jumps into action.
Explain these dark dreams, I dare you.
Why is difference so fearful?
Why does light attract and truth appal?
Ethereal flames rise through the sky
incinerating all our good intentions,

while my blood's earth
falls in love with its own weight.
Without darkness there is no light.
Without anvils there are no feathers.
Light confounds as much as it exalts.
One foot half on the ground
the other one half up in smoke.

Angophoras

The grinding stones beneath our boot heels
like teeth on honeycomb, as we stride
between angophoras, lunch sweating
in our backpacks, you dawdle, back there,
dissecting the irritable mystery of plucked
stamen having given up smoking ten hours
ago, you laugh at the leeches in my socks,
the knuckled warts and ganglions
of those wounded trunks, sap bleeding
red along the ridge, you extemporize,
make mythical their pink carnage
in the mist's deep silence, while I,
striding ahead at the gauntlet's end,
seeing nothing, commence the climb.

Egg Beater

You satellite!
Unearthed skeleton
all warts and bunions
whirring like a bicycle
at the scene of an accident.
Stop.
Let me extricate
my tongue
from your intricate
bones.

Bio Note

I was born and had a childhood.
Food passed through me and I grew.
My juvenile life was full of valuable learning experiences
such as Cuisenaire and potato prints.

I ran around and prospered.
I once fell out of a willow tree and was concussed for two weeks.
My first job was to buy Craven A's
from the corner milk bar for my mother.

The psychology of my sibling rivalry was far
more complex than my parents could figure.
Blindingly average rather than prodigy was I.
One or two significant teachers there were.

Adolescence was unremarkable, apart from the usual.
On the sporting field I excelled
which I know is hard to believe.
My second job was as a newsboy.

To be understood was not one of my ambitions.
As I grew older I grew happier,
or at least less disappointed.
I failed some tests and passed others.

My main personality trait I would describe as gullibility.
I loved and was loved, and for this I am grateful.
I reproduced.
I worked far more than I wanted

even though my instinct was not to.
I tried not to hurt others but in this I failed.
I influenced no one to the better.
I have been to many funerals.

Acknowledgements

Some of these poems have previously appeared, some in slightly different forms in: *Abridged* (Ireland), *Adelaide Literary Magazine* (USA), *Antipodes* (USA), *Australian Poetry Members Journal, The Best Australian Science Writing, Bluepepper, The Canberra Times, Cordite, Crannog* (Ireland), *The Enchanted Verses* (Ireland), *Famous Reporter, Four W, Griffith Review, Honest Ulsterman* (Ireland), *JAAM* (NZ), *Meanjin, Rabbit Poetry Journal, Scar* (ed. Cassandra Atherton, 2020), *Science Write Now, Seizure, Snorkel, Spindrift, Stilts, Stylus, Transnational Literature, Verity La.* Others have appeared in the chapbook *Shared Breath,* (Hope Street Press, 2017)

'Ludmilla's Cottage' was winner of the John Shaw Neilson Poetry Prize, 2016; 'Lines for Lyres' was short listed for the Newcastle Poetry Prize, 2016; 'Kite' was winner of the Melbourne Poets Union International Poetry Prize, 2017; 'Shackleton's Hut' was short listed for the Newcastle Poetry Prize, 2018; 'Communion of Stones' was highly commended in the WB Yeats Poetry Prize, 2016; 'Rat Nest' was broadcast on Little Fictions on Air, 2020; and 'Interesting Times' was winner of the Banjo Paterson Poetry Prize (open), 2021.

www.ingramcontent.com/pod-product-compliance
Lightning Source LLC
Chambersburg PA
CBHW031001090426
42737CB00008B/633